The Armadillo

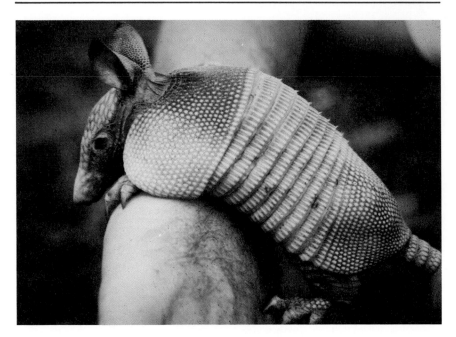

The Armadillo

By Seliesa Pembleton

DILLON PRESS
New York

Maxwell Macmillan Canada
Toronto

Maxwell Macmillan International
New York   Oxford   Singapore   Sydney

Acknowledgments

With thanks to Dr. Robert Baker, Horn Professor, Texas Tech University, for his assistance.

Photo Credits

Photo research by Debbie Needleman

Front and Back Covers courtesy of Dr. Tracy Carter

Interior: Texas Zoo, frontispiece; Dr. Tracy Carter, title page, 20, 23, 25, 35, 48; Louisiana Department of Wildlife and Fisheries, 8, 13, 41; Stephen Kirkpatrick, 11; Mark Mayfield/San Antonio Zoo, 14; Dr. Charles Steinmetz, Jr.: Photo/Nats, 16; Leonard Lee Rue III, 18, 43; Dr. Phillip Myers, 27; Florida Game and Fresh Water Fish Commission, 28, 46; Gillis W. Long Hansen's Disease Center, 30, 33, 38; Robin Doughty, 51; James Gaines/Florida Department of Commerce, 54

Library of Congress Cataloging-in-Publication Data

Pembleton, Seliesa.
    The armadillo / Seliesa Pembleton.
       p. cm. — (Remarkable animals)
    Summary: Describes the characteristics, habits, and life cycle of the nine-banded armadillo, called "turtle rabbit" by the Aztecs.
    ISBN 0-87518-507-X
    1. Armadillos—Juvenile literature. [1. Armadillos.] I. Title. II. Series: Dillon remarkable animals book.
QL737.E23P46   1992
599.3'1—dc20   91-43731

Dillon Press   Maxwell Macmillan Canada, Inc.
Macmillan Publishing Company   1200 Eglinton Avenue East
866 Third Avenue   Suite 200
New York, NY 10022   Don Mills, Ontario M3C 3N1

Macmillan Publishing Company is part of the Maxwell Communication Group of Companies.

First edition
Printed in the United States of America
10 9 8 7 6 5 4 3 2 1

Contents

Facts about
the Nine-banded Armadillo

Scientific Name: *Dasypus novemcinctus*

Description:

Length—Of head and body, 15 to 17 inches (38 to 43 centimeters); of tail, 14 to 16 inches (36 to 41 centimeters)

Weight—8 to 17 pounds (3.6 to 7.7 kilograms)

Physical Features—Body is shielded by bony pieces covered with leathery skin and sparse hairs. Eyes are small, ears are thin and covered with scaly skin. Nose is long and pointed. Teeth are in the rear of mouth only, and are small, peg shaped, and lack enamel covering. Long, pointed tail is covered with rings of scales. Legs are short and strong, with four toes on front paws and five toes on hind paws. Has large curved claws.

Color—Grayish with sparse, yellowish white hairs

Distinctive Habits: During the summer, spends most of the day sleeping in an underground burrow and comes out to eat at night. Reverses schedule in winter to hunt in warmest part of the afternoon. Uses claws and nose to root through dirt and fallen leaves in search of food. May jump straight up into the air when startled. Dashes to burrow or thick brush for safety.

Food: Mostly insects and other small invertebrates such as spiders, scorpions, and snails. Occasionally eats plant shoots, fruit, eggs, small snakes, and dead animals.

Reproductive Cycle: Begins breeding at one year of age. Mates in late summer or fall. Pups are born in March or April and are always identical and of the same sex. They are usually quadruplets. Pups remain with mother until she is ready to breed again.

Life Span: About ten years

Range: Southern United States, Mexico, Central America, and much of South America. Range is currently extending into North America.

Habitat: Woodlands with soft soil, brushy areas, and rocky outcrops

Related Species: There are 20 species in the armadillo family, ranging from the tiny pink fairy armadillo to the giant armadillo.

The areas in red show the range of the armadillo

7

Chapter 1

An Animal in Armor

It is almost dark when the strange-looking animal comes up out of a hole in the ground. In the woodland shadows its humped body looks like a rounded gray rock. The stocky creature is about the size of a large house cat, but its body is covered with bony armor. This hard protective covering gives the animal its name—*armadillo*.

As the armadillo shuffles noisily through the fallen leaves, its long, slender nose plows along the ground, sniffing for food. Suddenly, the armadillo smells dinner. With the long toenails on its front paws, the animal digs into a rotten log to uncover a tasty meal—a large scorpion.

The scorpion is ready to defend itself. It waves the claws on its front legs menacingly as it raises a long, jointed tail with a poison stinger on the tip. The hungry armadillo, however, quickly slurps up the scorpion with a long, slender, wet tongue. Not even the pincers and poison stinger of a scorpion can poke through an armored hide!

Its meal complete, the armadillo shuffles off again, then stops short when it hears a sound. Its beady eyes blink and its thin, leathery ears wiggle. A big dog is barking as it runs toward the armadillo.

Although the armadillo's back is covered with armor, a dog with strong jaws and sharp teeth could slash open its soft belly. On short legs, the small animal scurries toward a hole, but the long-legged dog is faster.

Trapped, the armadillo hunches down close to the ground. Then, just as the big dog opens its wide mouth, the frightened armadillo jumps straight up into the air like a jack-in-the-box!

With a yelp of pain, the stunned dog stumbles backward. The jumping armadillo has hit the dog in the mouth with its hard back. Quickly, the armadillo

Despite its armored coat, an armadillo must always be alert for predators.

dashes through the bushes and dives into the safety of its burrow.

The Protective Shield

In Spanish, the word *armadillo* means "little armored one." The name fits this remarkable animal perfectly: The armadillo is the only **mammal*** with a suit of bony armor.

* Words in **bold type** are explained in the glossary at the end of this book.

The nine-banded armadillo is covered on its back, sides, and tail with bony pieces that have a tough, scaly skin stretched over them. The armor across the animal's back is divided into three main regions. One large shield protects the armadillo's shoulders. It fits across the animal's body like a saddle. Another shield fits across the armadillo's hips. The middle of the back is shielded by a number of movable, bony bands. Usually nine in number (although sometimes there are eight, ten, or eleven), they are joined together by leathery skin that allows them to move somewhat like the folds of an accordion.

Behind its armored body, the animal drags a long, pointed tail. The tail is almost as long as the body and is protected by 12 bony, scale-covered rings. From the end of its nose to the tip of its tail, the nine-banded armadillo measures about 2½ feet (76 centimeters), and it can weigh up to 17 pounds (7.7 kilograms). Because its armor is heavy and bulky, the armadillo walks with a slow, jerky motion.

The armadillo's hard coat protects it from many

The armadillo's protective shield is divided into three sections.

predators, animals that would try to eat it. A young armadillo, however, is still in danger from predators, since its bony armor may be no thicker than a hard fingernail. The armor toughens and thickens as the animal grows older and larger. But the sharp fangs of a large dog, coyote, or cougar can sometimes bite into even the hard covering of an adult armadillo.

With its sharp sense of smell, an armadillo can sniff out insects deep within the ground.

A few hairs grow beside each scale along the nine-banded armadillo's back. The animal also has a beard of coarse, yellowish white hair on its chin. The underside of the armadillo has no armor. It is covered instead by a soft hide, or skin, with a few coarse white hairs.

A Long Nose and Few Teeth

A scaly helmet protects the armadillo's head. The animal has thin ears, with a tough, pebbly surface, and two small black eyes. But the armadillo does not see or hear very well. It depends instead on its amazingly keen sense of smell.

With the long, pink, piglike nose wriggling on the end of its pointed face, the nine-banded armadillo can smell a meal as deep as eight inches (20 centimeters) underground! The animal uses its snout to push through dirt and fallen leaves as it sniffs for food.

The armadillo eats mostly meat. Its favorite foods are insects, especially beetles and ants. But it will also gobble up worms, spiders, scorpions, small snakes and lizards, and an occasional bird or egg.

Surprisingly, the armadillo eats all these foods without the help of any teeth at all in the front of its mouth. It has just a few—from seven to nine—small, peglike teeth in the back of its upper and lower jaws. The armadillo does not need fangs or big teeth, because it doesn't depend on its teeth for protection.

The armadillo can dig its way to safety in a matter of minutes.

It has a suit of armor for that.

The few teeth the armadillo does have are un-usual, however. They lack the hard protective **enamel** covering that most animals have on their teeth. But armadillos don't chew their food very much.

When it eats, the armadillo uses its hard, worm-like tongue and its thick, sticky **saliva** more than it uses its teeth. As the hungry armadillo eats, its mouth fills with saliva. The long, thin tongue, wet with saliva, flicks in and out—as far as three inches beyond the mouth. The gluey liquid on the tongue traps insects and other small creatures. Then the armadillo may even use its tough tongue to help mash the food before it is swallowed.

The "Disappearing" Armadillo

The armadillo has a remarkable ability to dig quickly. With this skill, it can "disappear" fast when threatened by a hungry predator. While a nine-banded armadillo may try to curl up to protect its underside, it cannot roll into a tight ball. It would rather escape into a quickly dug hole.

The nine-banded armadillo has four toes on its front paws and five toes on its hind paws. The two toes in the center of the paws have long, curved claws that are good for digging. With these curved claws and its short but strong front legs, an armadillo often can dig a hole fast enough to seem to disappear into

An armadillo will sometimes try to protect itself by curling up.

the ground before its surprised enemy.

Even a shallow hole can provide protection. Although its hard, curved back may stick up out of the sand, an armadillo can bury its soft, unarmored belly in the dirt.

A predator may be in for a surprise when it attacks the armored back sticking up out of the earth.

18

A frightened armadillo can jump as high as three feet (0.9 meter) straight up into the air. The hungry predator may be so startled that the armadillo has a few seconds to escape. If it gets hit in the mouth, the predator may even end up with a dislocated jaw instead of a meal.

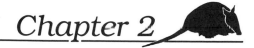

Chapter 2

The Nine-banded Armadillo and Its Relatives

The nine-banded armadillo is also known as the long-nosed armadillo. In Spanish-speaking countries, it is called *tatus*, *armado*, or *mulita*. It is puzzling when one kind of animal has so many different names.

To help clear up this confusion, scientists have developed an organized way of studying and naming living things. Each creature is given a two-part Latin or Greek name, which usually gives clues about what the animal is like. No matter what language they speak, all scientists around the world use

The greater naked-tail armadillo, one of the 20 different kinds of armadillos.

21

this two-part name when they refer to a certain animal.

Dasypus novemcinctus is the name scientists have given to the nine-banded armadillo. "Dasypus" is the Latin word for an old Aztec Indian name that means "turtle-rabbit." The armadillo's bony armor reminded the Aztecs of a turtle, and its long ears made them think of a rabbit.

"Novemcinctus" is a combination of two words. In Latin, "novem" means nine, and "cinctus" means cinch or band. Together, these words tell us that this type of armadillo has nine bands of armor across the middle of its back.

As part of their organized method of studying living things, scientists **classify,** or group, animals together according to their similar characteristics. All of the animals that have hair, are warm blooded, and feed milk to their babies are called mammals. Armadillos are mammals.

Some mammals have sharp, meat-tearing teeth, while others have flattened teeth used for grinding. Scientists put armadillos, anteaters, and **sloths** into a

The Aztec Indians called the armadillo a "turtle-rabbit" because of its long ears and hard shell.

smaller group of mammals called **Edentata**, which means "toothless." Anteaters have no teeth at all. Armadillos and sloths have bare gums in the front of their mouths and a few small teeth along the back of their jaws.

The Edentata are among the most **primitive**, or least developed, mammals in North and South America, and armadillos are the most primitive of the Edentata. Armadillos have been on earth for about 55 million years.

Of the three kinds of Edentata, only armadillos have an armor coat. Because of this, scientists put them into a **family** by themselves. There are 20 different kinds, or **species**, of armadillos. Some are very much like the nine-banded armadillo. Some, including the giant armadillo, the pink fairy, and the three-banded armadillo, are very different.

The Giant Armadillo

At two o'clock one morning, a research scientist camping out in Brazil was startled by loud noises. A large animal came crashing through the dark tangle of jungle vines. The scientist sat very still as the humpbacked creature stumbled into the moonlit clearing. As the animal came toward him, the man could see long claws on its paws.

But the creature did not threaten the scientist. Instead, with its long pink nose wriggling back and forth, it walked right up and sniffed his legs

With its huge claws, this armadillo can dig a burrow large enough to hold a human being.

and boots. Then the armored animal turned and shuffled away into the darkness.

This scientist had just met the largest member of the armadillo family. Giant armadillos can grow to more than 4 feet (1.2 meters) long and weigh as much as 130 pounds (59 kilograms)—about three times longer and 7½ times heavier than the biggest nine-banded armadillos.

Giant armadillos have huge claws—up to 8 inches (20.5 centimeters) long—which they use for digging. The burrow a giant armadillo digs is so large that a small person can crawl into it.

Because they dig such big holes and like to eat maggots and other insects that feed on dead animals—and sometimes the dead animals, too—these giants are also called grave-digger armadillos.

The Tiny Pink Fairy

The pink fairy armadillo is small and rare. From the tip of its nose to the tip of its tail, this tiny cousin of the nine-banded armadillo is only about 7 inches (17.9 centimeters) long. It has pale pink armor, and its sides and belly are covered with fine, soft, white hairs. This makes the pink fairy armadillo look like a small guinea pig with armor on its back.

The pink fairy's tail is a piece of broad, flat armor. When the tiny armadillo crawls into its burrow, it can use its armored rear to plug the burrow opening, much like a cork in a bottle!

Only the three-banded armadillo can totally curl up into a tight ball.

The Three-banded Armadillo

The three-banded armadillo is the only kind of armadillo that can roll up completely into a tight ball for protection. The large shields at the front and back of its body are not connected to skin on the sides of the body. This allows the animal to pull its legs inside its bony shell when it is threatened. At the same time, it curls its head and tail inward. The armored tail and the helmet on the head close the space between the large shields, forming a round shape. Very few predators have the strength to pry open this hard, tight ball.

Chapter 3

Home Is Where the Hole Is

Armadillos like soft soil, warm weather, and ants or other insects to eat. The perfect armadillo **habitat**, or home, has all three of these—plus water to drink and some thick, thorny bushes to scurry into for safety.

Soft soil is important to an animal that searches for food by plowing through the dirt with its nose and uses its claws to dig a home in the ground. Armadillos can live in rocky areas only if there are cracks between the rocks where they can make dens.

Armadillos dig more holes than most other **burrowing** mammals. These burrows serve many purposes. A deep burrow shelters the armadillo not only from predators, but also from very cold weather in the winter and very hot weather in the summer. A shallow burrow provides a hideout for the armadillo

A nine-banded armadillo at home in the woodlands.

An armadillo's burrow protects it not only from other animals, but also from very hot or very cold temperatures.

when danger is near. The armadillo digs several shallow burrows in the area where it lives. Then it can dart quickly to safety in a nearby hole.

Burrows are also good places for the armadillo to look for food. Many small animals that cannot dig a hole easily take shelter in empty armadillo burrows. These creatures do risk, however, being eaten by a hungry predator. Not only armadillos but foxes, coyotes, raccoons, skunks, and other animals often stop to check for food in abandoned armadillo burrows.

A Warm Climate

The climate in an area helps determine what kinds of animals can live there. Armadillos have no fur to keep them warm, and their bodies are not very good at creating heat when the outside temperature drops. In very cold climates, the animal can suffer frostbite or even freeze to death. Armadillos seldom survive in a place where the temperature drops below 32° Fahrenheit (0° Celsius) for nine days or more.

Some animals survive in cold climates by **hibernating**, or spending the winter in a sleeplike condition inside a den. Instead of eating, hibernating animals use stored body fat for energy. But armadillos do not hibernate. No matter how cold it gets, the armadillo must leave its den to search for food.

If the ground near the armadillo's burrow is frozen hard, the animal's nose can't plow through the

31

soil, and the insects or other food will be hidden or frozen, too. The unlucky armadillo may find little or nothing to eat. Then it starves to death!

Armadillos live only in warmer climates, where the winters are mild. The warmer climate of the southern United States and the tropical climate of Mexico and Central and South America make these areas good places for armadillos to live.

When the weather is hot in the summer, the armadillo sleeps in its hole during the day, because the damp earth is much cooler than the outside air. The animal will come out to eat at night, when many small creatures are busy crawling along the ground. Animals such as the armadillo that sleep during the day and are active at night are called **nocturnal**.

But when the cold winter winds blow, the armadillo reverses its schedule. It stays snuggled in its burrow during the frosty night and comes out to feed in the warmest part of the afternoon. Then it is called **diurnal**, which means it is active during the day.

In years when the winters are mild and the

An armadillo usually sleeps during the day and comes out of its burrow at night to hunt for food.

ground is frozen for only a few nights, armadillos may move farther north to dig their burrows. Sometimes the armadillos that move farthest north have the tips of their ears frozen off during a cold spell. When the winters become harsh, these pioneering armadillos must move back south or shiver and die in a cold hole in the ground.

Nine-banded Armadillos on the Move

Of all the armadillos, the nine-banded armadillos have the largest **range**, or geographic area in which they can be found. Other types of armadillos live mainly in Central and South America. But nine-banded armadillos live as far south as northern Argentina and as far north as Kansas in the United States. They can be found from the American Southwest to the Atlantic coast.

Nine-banded armadillos haven't always lived in the United States. They've moved northward from Mexico. In the 1850s, about the time that Texas became a state, the armadillos crossed the Rio Grande River from Mexico into Texas. But how did these heavy, hard-shelled animals get across the Rio Grande?

The nine-banded armadillo has an amazing way of crossing water. If a stream is narrow, the armadillo takes a deep breath and walks across the bottom of the river, like a moving rock. The animal can hold its breath for up to six minutes. To cross a wider river, the armadillo gulps air into its stomach and intes-

34

This armadillo has no trouble crossing a stream.

tines and then floats or paddles across. When crossing a wide, fast river, armadillos will cling to pieces of floating wood.

After they crossed the Rio Grande, the nine-banded armadillos traveled north into Texas by following the riverbanks, where there was plenty of water. They dug new homes in the soft, sandy soil.

When plants or animals move into a new area, scientists call them **invaders**—these armadillos were invading Texas!

Over the next hundred years, the armored pioneers spread out. They moved west as far as the west Texas plains. They moved north to Oklahoma, southern Kansas, and Arkansas. They moved east until they reached Louisiana and the mighty, muddy Mississippi River.

In 1922, a small boy in Florida found an armadillo and brought it to a zoo. Scientists were amazed. How did the stubby-legged creature get so far? With a little detective work, a scientist at the zoo solved the mystery.

A soldier from Texas who was stationed in south Florida during World War I had brought a pair of pet armadillos with him. After the war ended, the soldier turned his pets loose before returning home.

Florida had soft, sandy soil, warm winters, and plenty of insects. The pair of armadillos found it a perfect place to live. They mated and multiplied quickly. Soon nine-banded armadillos lived in all of Florida except the swamps, where it was too wet to dig holes. Then they began to move northward toward Georgia.

Now, armadillos live in Georgia, Alabama, and Mississippi, too. Every year, these armored invaders travel farther into North America, and the area they call home grows larger and larger.

No one knows exactly why the nine-banded armadillo has been such a successful pioneer. Perhaps it is because there are few natural predators left where the armadillos live. People have either killed or chased away most of the coyotes, wolves, bobcats, and cougars that once were the armadillo's main enemies. Some scientists think that winters in the northern United States are becoming warmer, making the region safe for armadillos. Whatever the reason, nine-banded armadillos are still on the move.

Chapter 4

An Armadillo Year

Spring

It is a gray April evening. Raindrops splatter on the rocks and soak into the brown dirt. Water begins to seep into a burrow.

A pregnant nine-banded armadillo has spent the winter living in this den, near a creek flowing through the Arkansas woodland. Now the burrow is turning wet and muddy. The armadillo must move away from the creek to higher, drier ground. She needs a safe place to bear her young.

The first thing the armadillo does when she comes up out of the burrow is to look for food. After sleeping, she is hungry. The animal makes soft grunting noises as she searches the ground. Her wet tongue slurps up termites in a rotten log, and she gobbles a

In the spring, as the ground turns soft and wet,
armadillos look for new, dry spots to dig their burrows.

tarantula that was hiding under a rock.

As the armadillo waddles uphill, she pushes her hard body through a clump of bushes with sharp thorns and thick branches. The thorns can't hurt her tough hide. This is the right spot to dig a new home, where the tangle of thorns will help protect the entrance.

Her curved claws work like little shovels to scoop out the wet earth. Deeper and deeper the animal digs. Then she stops to rest.

For about 120 days, babies have been growing inside the armadillo's swollen body. Last July she mated with a larger, male armadillo that found her by following her scent trail. After mating, she and the male went their separate ways. Armadillos usually live alone, except when a mother is raising her young, and then she has the babies for company. After mating, the babies began to develop inside the mother's body. Then, for some reason scientists do

A female armadillo usually gives birth to four pups of the same sex—and they look exactly alike.

not completely understand, the babies stopped growing for about 14 weeks. After this "resting" period, the babies started to grow again. Now they are ready to be born.

Birth of the Babies

When the rain stops and the grass near the burrow is dry, the armadillo begins to make a bed in the large hollow she has scooped out at one end of the burrow. To do this, she bunches dry grass and leaves between her front and hind legs and then hops backward down into the hole. It takes many trips down the dark tunnel to make a fluffy place to sleep.

Soon, tiny, wriggling bodies snuggle in the underground den. The armadillo has given birth to four female babies.

These babies, called pups, are identical **quadruplets**. They are all the same sex and size, and they look just alike. An armadillo **litter** is always either all male or all female, and there are usually four babies.

The pink armor on the lively little pups is smooth, soft, and shiny. It feels somewhat like a wax coating. It will become darker, harder, and thicker as the animals grow larger. Right now, a pup is small enough to sit in the palm of a person's hand.

Unlike many newborn mammals, the armadillo pups can open their bright black eyes immediately. Within a few hours, they will be strong enough to walk. In a few weeks, they will go with their mother

An armadillo pup—its shiny pink armor is still soft.

as she hunts for food. But for now, they play and sleep inside the den and drink their mother's milk.

The mother armadillo leaves the burrow each evening at dark to search for her own meals and to dig some shallow burrows. When the pups are old enough to travel with her at night, they will have these other holes to flee to if trouble approaches.

Summer

In June, the days are long and warm. The armadillo family spends each day napping in the cool burrow. The pups are almost as large as their mother now, and they eat the same foods she does. At night, they make a lot of noise as they all shuffle through the moist dirt and leaves searching for food.

By July, the strong, young armadillos roam farther and farther from their mother as they hunt. In a couple of weeks, when it is time for the mother to mate again, she will chase her youngsters from the burrow. Then each will dig a den of its own.

Fall

On the first frosty fall day, one of the young armadillos comes out to hunt while the sun is shining. The animal no longer sleeps all day and hunts at night. Instead, it stays snuggled in its burrow during the cold night and comes out to feed during the warmest part of the day. That is when insects are most likely to be crawling.

This afternoon, however, a meal is hard to find. The ants are deep inside the anthills. Beetles and centipedes have burrowed away for the winter. The armadillo roots through the frosty leaves and cold dirt but uncovers nothing to eat.

The animal heads toward one of the safety holes it dug late this summer. What luck—several large crickets are hanging upside down from the roof of the burrow. The long-tongued armadillo won't go hungry today.

Winter

The easiest part of an armadillo's year is over. Now a real struggle begins.

Arkansas winters are usually mild, but this is about as far north as an armadillo can live. In an unusual year when the ground is frozen for weeks, the armadillos are in big trouble.

On an afternoon at the end of February, one of the young armadillos digs around a pile of wood. As its front claws rip away the soft, rotten wood, it finds a

A young armadillo comes out to root in the springtime sun.

cold, slow-moving lizard hidden underneath. The lizard will be the armadillo's last meal for several days. A snowstorm is on the way.

For the next two days, the temperature is below freezing. The armadillos huddle in their dens. They tuck their heads between their front legs and shiver in the cold, snow-covered earth.

Signs of Spring

On the third day after the storm, the sun rises in a clear sky. The temperature warms to 40°F (4.4°C), and the snow begins to melt. Hungry armadillos come out to root through the thawing dirt.

This first day of March brings signs of spring—small yellow flowers appear on the branches of witch hazel trees. Soon, the warmer earth will be crawling with insects.

The young armadillos who survived the winter are almost a year old. This summer, each will be ready to mate and raise a litter of four new pups to take their place in the armadillo's yearly cycle of cold and warm seasons. Another armadillo year has begun.

Chapter 5

Armadillos and People

In North America, many of the armadillo's natural predators, such as bobcats and cougars, have become scarce. Today, people pose the most problems for the armadillo, but they are not a real threat to the animal's existence.

Armadillos do get hit by cars. At night, when the animals are out searching for food, even a watchful driver may not see an armadillo until it is very close. As the driver tries to avoid hitting the animal, the frightened armadillo reacts as it usually does when a big predator is near. It leaps straight up into the air. Sometimes it hits the underside of the car and is killed.

A six-banded armadillo hitches a ride on a friend.

An Affection for Armadillos

Most people would never harm this remarkable animal on purpose. In fact, many people are very fond of armadillos. Sometimes they keep them as pets— even though they often find that armadillos are not perfect houseguests.

"Armadillos are fun to watch, but they don't make very good pets," said a Texan who kept one in a fenced yard. "It's no fun to pet an armadillo or hold it on your lap. Besides, it sleeps all day and comes out at night, when you are ready to go to bed," the man added. "And phew, it smells like an old pair of gym shoes, too! So after a while, I turned the armadillo loose."

People who move to a new home with their pet armadillo and then turn the animal loose when they grow tired of it help armadillos spread into new areas.

Some people raise armadillos for food. Armadillo meat is a favorite food for many people in the southern United States and in Latin America. It is tender and white, and it tastes like pork. The meat is

Armadillo hides drying in the Texas sun. For years they have been used to make baskets and handbags.

usually roasted or barbecued in the "shell." The hard armadillo hide is sometimes used to make baskets or handbags.

In spite of the fact that people use armadillos for food and other products, there are more armadillos in the United States now than there used to be.

Many farmers and gardeners like armadillos

because the animals eat fire ants, beetles, and other insect pests. If these insects weren't eaten, they might munch on the flowers and vegetables the people were trying to grow.

Armadillos also are useful to scientists who are looking for a cure for a disease called leprosy. Leprosy is a dreaded and contagious disease that attacks the skin and nerves. It has plagued people since ancient times. It causes lumps, oozing sores, and white, peeling scabs. It may even cause body parts such as an ear to wither and die.

It was hard for scientists to learn much about leprosy until they discovered that some armadillos also die from leprosy. Now that they know armadillos are victims, too, doctors are studying the disease in armadillos. Perhaps someday this study will help them find a cure.

A Texas Good Luck Symbol

In 1978, students at Oak Creek Elementary School in Houston, Texas, decided that the nine-banded armadillo should become the official Texas state mammal. The state already had an official state bird, flower, and tree. "Why not a mammal, too?" the children asked.

For three years, students, parents, teachers, and community leaders worked to have the Texas government pass a law making the armadillo the state mammal. They had a hard job, because not everyone loved armadillos.

Some ranchers claimed armadillo holes were unsafe for cattle, which could break their legs if they stumbled into the holes. But other people argued that most armadillo holes are in bushy areas or around the roots of trees, where cattle seldom walk.

Some farmers and gardeners complained that armadillos mess up lawns or root through crops. Perhaps these people had never thought about all the good armadillos do when they eat insect pests.

Some hunters said they didn't like armadillos because the animals eat the eggs of wild game birds such as turkey and quail. The hunters feared they would have fewer birds to shoot. But scientists who

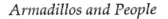

studied the eating habits of armadillos found that armadillos only occasionally eat eggs.

In 1981, the children at Oak Creek School had a reason to celebrate. Although the government did not make the nine-banded armadillo the state mammal, the popular animal was declared the official state mascot, a good-luck symbol for Texans.

The Popular Armadillo

Every year there are more and more nine-banded armadillos in the United States. And they are very popular, too. Some people even like to race them. All over the country, pictures of armadillos can be seen on T-shirts, television commercials, souvenirs, toys, and belt buckles.

What makes this unusual animal so popular? Perhaps people admire its hardiness—the way it has survived and moved into new territories. Perhaps they are grateful for its usefulness in studying leprosy. Or maybe they just like the look of this remarkable animal with the armor coat.

An armadillo race in Orlando, Florida.

Glossary

burrowing—digging holes, or burrows, for shelter

classify—to arrange living things into groups according to their relationships. One system of classification puts all living things into five groups, called kingdoms: plants, animals, bacteria, fungi (FUN-jy), and Protista (one-celled living things). The kingdoms are divided into groups. Each group is smaller than the previous group: phylum, class, order, family, genus, and species.

diurnal (die-URN-ul)—active during the day. When the weather is very cold, the armadillo sleeps in its burrow at night and hunts for food during the day.

Edentata (ee-DEN-tah-tah)—a group (order) of related animals with similar characteristics, including a lack of teeth in the front of the mouth. Anteaters, sloths, and armadillos are in this group.

enamel—the smooth, hard, shiny outer covering of a tooth

family—a word used by scientists in classifying living things. A family is a group of similar animals or plants from a particular order.

habitat (HAB-ih-tat)—the area where a plant or animal naturally lives and grows

hibernate (HIGH-bur-nate)—to spend the winter in a

sleeplike, inactive condition. The animal's heartbeat and breathing slow down, and instead of eating, the animal uses stored body fat for its energy.

invasion—when a large number of plants or animals begin to grow or live in an area where they have not lived before. Plants or animals living in the new region are called invaders.

leprosy (LEP-ruh-see)—a contagious disease of the skin and nerves that causes sores, white scaly scabs, and deformities. Leprosy is known to infect only humans and armadillos.

litter—all the babies born at the same time to the same mother

mammal—a group (class) of warm-blooded animals that have backbones and hair. Female mammals have glands that produce milk, which they feed to their young.

nocturnal (knock-TER-nul)—active at night. The armadillo is a nocturnal animal that, in warm months, sleeps during the day and looks for food at night.

predator (PRED-uh-tuhr)—an animal that hunts other animals for food

primitive (PRIM-ih-tiv)—from an ancient period of time and not very well developed

quadruplets (kwah-DREW-plits)—four babies born to the same mother at the same time

range—the geographic area in which a kind of animal may be found. The nine-banded armadillo ranges from north-western Argentina and Uruguay through Central America and Mexico and into the southern United States.

saliva (suh-LIE-vuh)—a colorless, watery liquid that wets the inside of the mouth and helps in chewing, swallow-ing, and digesting food

sloth—a slow-moving South American mammal that spends much of its time hanging upside down from the branches of trees

species (SPEE-sheez)—a word used by scientists in classify-ing living things. A species is a group of animals or plants that have similar characteristics.

Index

About the Author

Seliesa Pembleton has a master of science degree in education and has taught students of all ages from elementary school through college.

In recent years, she has written "hands-on" science curriculums, teachers' aides, and student manuals for the National Science Resources Center, which is cosponsored by the National Academy of Sciences and the Smithsonian Institution. She is also the author of *The Pileated Woodpecker*, another book in the REMARKABLE ANIMALS series.

Ms. Pembleton is currently director of environmental studies at Hard Bargain Farm Environmental Center, located on the banks of the Potomac River near Washington, D.C. She enjoys helping children discover their relationship to the land—and to all the creatures that share it.